Letter To Myself

Kait Fedor

Presentation by *BookLeaf Publishing*

Web: www.bookleafpub.com

E-mail: info@bookleafpub.com

ISBN: 9789357740487

First edition 2023

To My Brothers, My Parents, and AMA+UW.

ACKNOWLEDGEMENT

Thank you to my family, my group, and all the English teachers who encouraged me to continue writing when I presented pure garbage for assignments.

PREFACE

There are references to heavy topics including: Trauma, Sexual Assault, Violence, and complicated relationships. Please don't go further if these are triggers for you. Your mental and physical well being come first!

Truth

Truth
The feeling of peaceful waves in a tsunami
The sound of angry shouts resolved
The vision of a heart healing
The taste of arriving home from a long escape
The smell of narcissus in the garden air
Truth is the blood in my veins
Thud…
      Thud…
         Thudding…
In my throat
Choking on my lies
Drowning me in
Truth

Pressure

Tension comes surface
Bubbles preparing to burst
Rage brings explosion

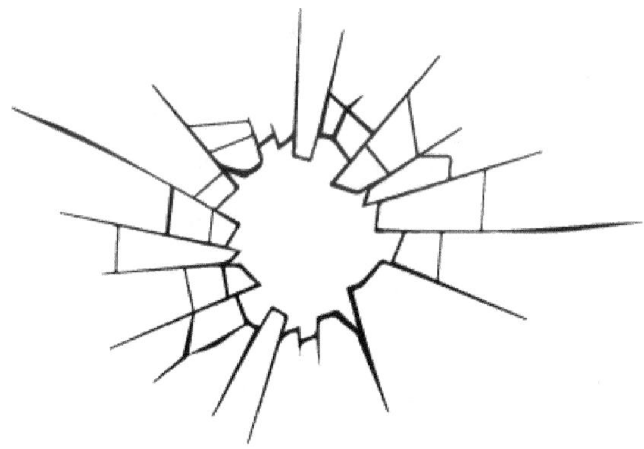

Survival of the Fittest

Aren't you tired?
I am.
Tired of holding you together
Tired of trying to keep you alive
Tired of breaking myself for you
I'm tired of saving you over myself
You get chances.
I get none.

I am quiet while you explode
I am invisible while you light up the room red
I am the strength while you are weak
I am the life raft while you choose to drown
I am exhausted in the wake of you.

I want to choose me
I want to save myself
I want to escape.
But I can't save us both this time.
I am not the glass that shatters under your
weight anymore
I am a raging wildfire burning us to the ground.

1 in 4.

Bile rising
In my throat.
Touch lingers
Choking my
Hope.

Still images
Light up my mind
Using my fears
Turned reality

Wanting to fight the
Hold on my body
Or the hands
Ravaging me
Eternally

Stop. Stop. STOP.
Ugly statistics add another
Rape. Another
Victim.
I refuse to be defined by
Vile numbers. I am one of the
Endless survivors.

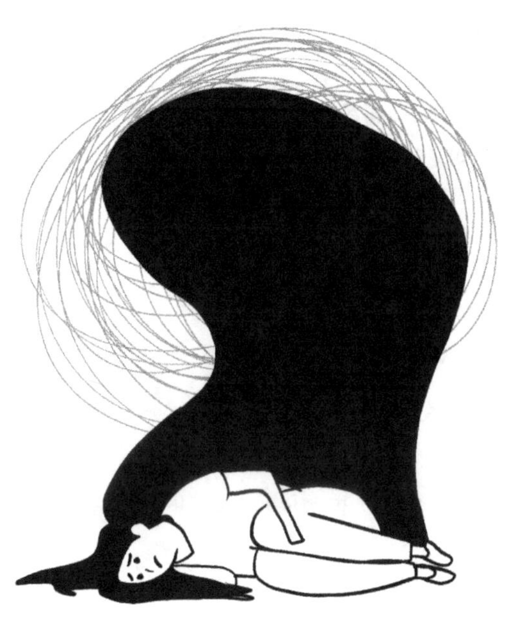

Art for the Artist

She wears shiny Doc Martens
Adorned with rainbow laces.
Chews on an art pen
As she sketches out our faces.

I watch her forehead crinkle,
Pen darting around.
Eyes start to twinkle,
Notebook unbound.

She says not a word,
Just quietly sighs,
While I think how absurd
For my feelings to arise

We sit together in silence, thinking what could
be wrong
as I watch my Artist give me a place to belong.

Forgotten Sacrifice

Sacrificed my heart.
She wanted another's love.
Forgotten heartbreak

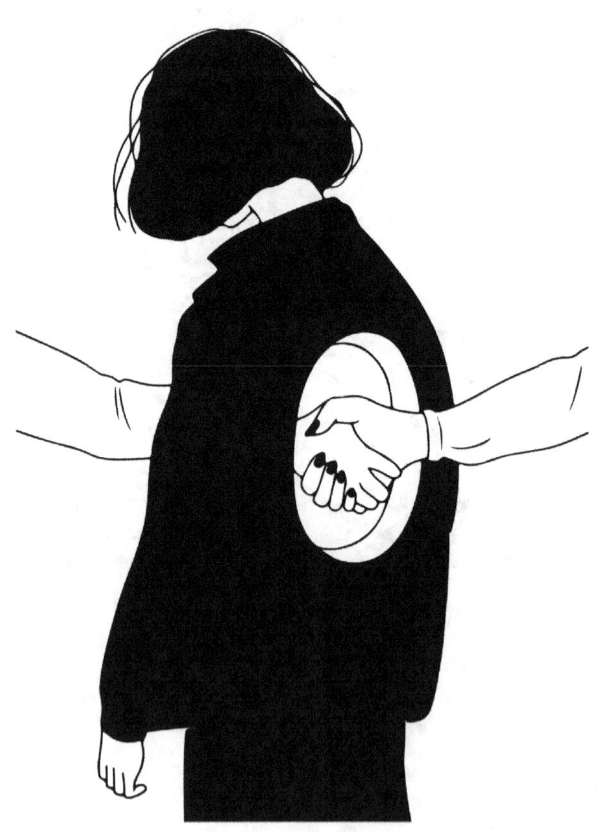

To The Mother

Left alone, death stick over family
Selfish and Selfless, two sides the same.
Chosen Addiction.
Smoking over kids.
Rumors and Lies left in your wake
Not meant for a child to navigate.
Sickness within led to silent rot
Family built, destroyed in the wake.
I resent and absolve you all the same.

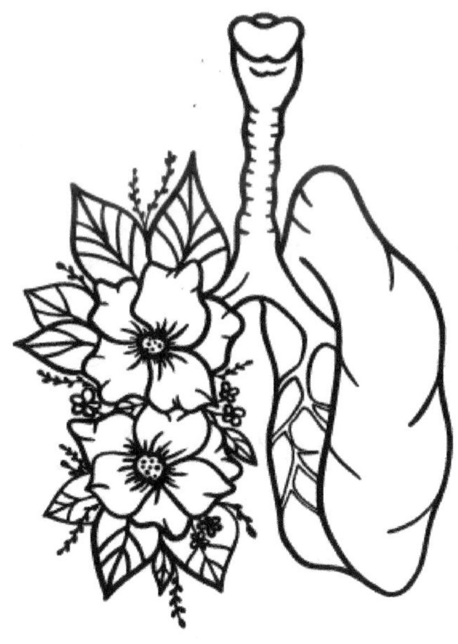

Fly Free

Staring out the window
Dreaming of freedom others have
They will never understand why
All I want to do is fly,
Fly far away,
And never look back.
I'm tired of being trapped
in my own private cage.
Gleaming from a glance.
Suffocation within.

Caged Bird

Just be grateful for your life
Everything handed to you without need,
Castle, Money, Power to boot.
Bars for Protection
Kept safe from the world
Trapped is the bird in the cage
Freedom is found in our home.
Staying secure in this place.

Intrusion

All that lays
Before my mind.

Chaos awakens
Darkening my soul,
Eating my heart
Feasting on pain.

Gripping my fears
Hatred burns and festers
I can't maintain a calm.

Judgment comes
Keeping me
Locked in the tsunami.

Manipulating my thoughts
Numbing the world
Offering silence
Perpetuating rage.

Quarantining myself.
Running from friends who
Supported me
Through the illness

Until there is nothing left.
Virtually unrecognizable
Without noticing.

Xanadu left me.
Yearning for
Zen, but still forsaken.

Lost

I wanted the win
Didn't care about the cost.
Whatever it took
Without thinking what I lost
Broken from the ghost of her.

Grey

I wanted to feel
The good and the bad
Vibrant colors and clear shapes.

Instead there is grey.
The world static and fuzzy
Like a tv with no source.

How can one thrive
If there is nothing in focus
If I'm left floating in oblivion.

She

There was a story I heard once
About a girl and a boy.
They fell for each other
Young and in love.

Until she discovered
A side of herself
Hidden from all
Until she was safe

She fell in love
With the girl of her dreams
Moment by moment
Step by step

Tattoo

Living drawings
Traced across
My canvas of skin
Carving their place
In my story
Just as they have
for centuries
Snapshots of memories
Moments to savor
Ink seeping deep
From skin to soul

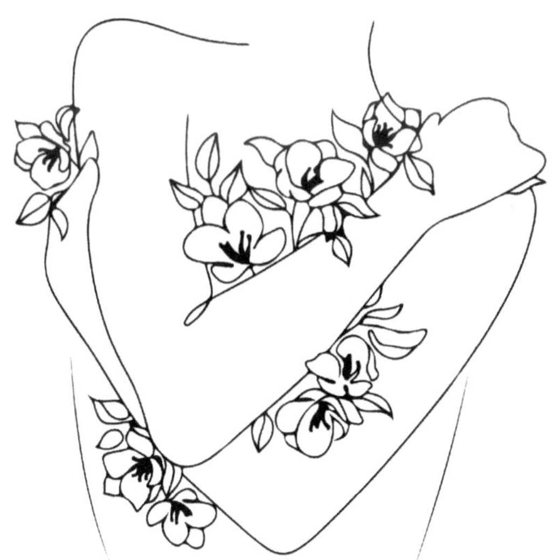

Toxic

Desire to escape
Toxicity surrounds me
Running from "home"

Loveless

Loveless
Does not mean that I love less.
I take each day with a full heart
watching the world forget to love
As greed and power poisons
All the love there should be.
I stand alone, a passerby

The love bleeds from my weeping eyes
Pouring tears into the ground
Hoping I can plant a new love
For the next loveless to come around
The one who knows
It is those who Love Less
That are truly loveless

Campground Peace

Chirping…
The crickets speak
A language all their own
Echoing throughout the campgrounds
Sleep comes

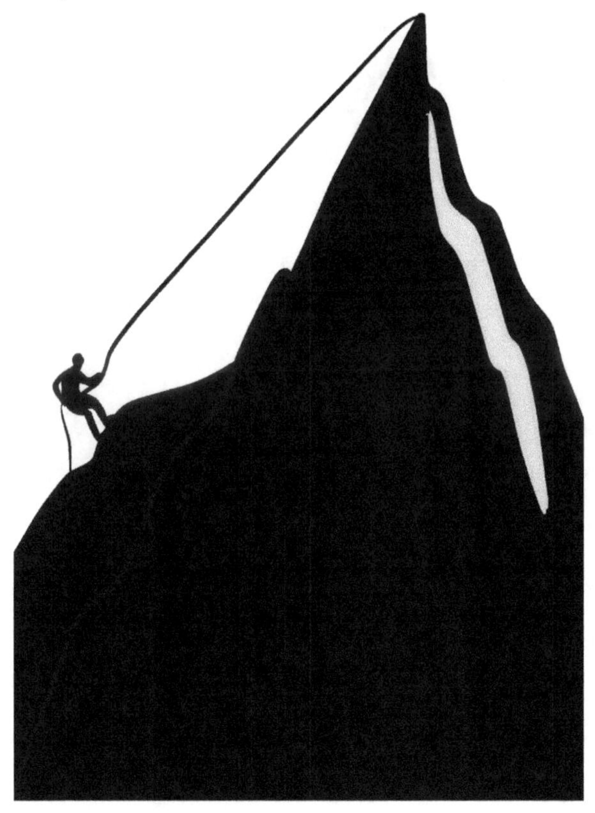

Spell for Healing

Healing scars of old
Hoping for internal change
Blossoming of new

Scream

I scream into oblivion, looking for some peace,
While my heart begs for tranquil silence
Anxiety wraps around my ribs, unable to cease
I scream into oblivion, looking for some peace,
My echoes sound of sorrow, incapable of release
The forest surrounds me showing defiance.
I scream into oblivion, looking for some peace,
While my heart begs for tranquil silence.

Home

Discovering who I am
Learning who I lost
Leaving the life I had
Embracing the life I want
Choosing a better outcome
Reflecting on the past
Searching for my inner peace
Finding what I need
I am home at last

A Letter to Myself

Dear Me,

I'm sorry that you suffered,
I live with that each day.
I wish what I discovered
Could take the pain away

You never deserved to feel
unwanted or alone.
I hope that we can heal
Cause we're stronger than you've known.

I can't change your future
Any more than my past.
But you will get here sooner
Than I possibly could have asked.

And one day when you write this
You'll look back at how life was.
I hope that you can find the bliss
Instead of all the cons.

In the end, I just want you to know
I'm proud to watch you grow